COSTUME

Accessories & Adornment

Helen Whitty
POWERHOUSE MUSEUM

Heinemann
LIBRARY

www.heinemann.co.uk/library
Visit our website to find out more information about **Heinemann Library** books.

To order:
 Phone 44 (0) 1865 888066
 Send a fax to 44 (0) 1865 314091
 Visit the Heinemann Bookshop at www.heinemann.co.uk/library to browse our catalogue and order online.

First published in Great Britain in 2001 by Heinemann Library, Halley Court, Jordan Hill, Oxford OX2 8EJ, a division of Reed Educational and Professional Publishing Ltd. Heinemann is a registered trademark of Reed Educational & Professional Publishing Limited.

OXFORD MELBOURNE AUCKLAND JOHANNESBURG BLANTYRE
GABORONE IBADAN PORTSMOUTH NH (USA) CHICAGO

First published 2000 by
MACMILLAN EDUCATION AUSTRALIA PTY LTD
627 Chapel Street, South Yarra, Australia 3141

Cover designed by Joanna Sapwell
Interior designed by Polar Design Pty Ltd
Illustrated by Wendy Arthur
Printed in China

ISBN 0 431 14424 9 (hardback)   ISBN 0 431 14431 1 (paperback)
05 04 03 02 01   05 04 03 02 01
10 9 8 7 6 5 4 3 2 1   10 9 8 7 6 5 4 3 2 1

British Library Cataloguing in Publication Data

Whitty, Helen
    Accessories and adornment. – (Costume)
    1. Dress accessories
    I. Title
    391.4'4

Cover photographs reproduced with permission of Powerhouse Museum, Sydney, Australia; and Utopia Art, Australia (necklaces).

Any words appearing in the text in bold, **like this**, are explained in the Glossary.

Contents

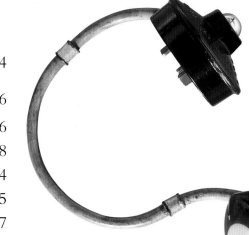

Don't turn this page!
Think of all the little things you wear, carry or attach to yourself. See if you recognize any of them in this book.

Introduction

The things you wear on your body are your costume. You probably have things you like to wear and things you have to wear. Your family probably likes you to wear special clothes for certain occasions. Sometimes what you like to wear and what your family wants you to wear are very different. Have you heard someone say, 'I wouldn't be caught dead in that dress/jacket/hat/shoes'? People can feel very strongly about what they, and others, wear.

▼ 'FUNK INC' poster from funkessentials, designed in 1993

The story of costume is about people's creativity and the ways they like to show it. What people make, wear and care about are examples of this creativity. What people wear says something about them. *Costume* looks at wearing and making clothes across times, places and cultures.

Don't get dressed up to read this book – just dust off your imagination. Start off by imagining yourself without costume.

Too revealing? The strange thing is, the more you cover up with costume, the more you are really saying about yourself.

▶ Transparent plastic figure of a woman. It is full size, and shows the body organs, veins and arteries. It was made in 1954 to teach people about health and hygiene.

▲ A necklace made of painted leather, 1925–45

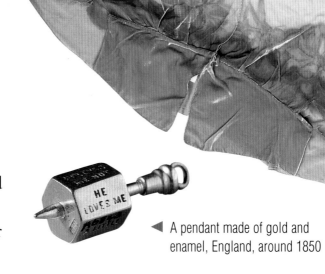

► A hand-painted silk shawl, 1920–30

Accessories and adornment

Accessories and Adornment looks at the many trinkets, art works, machines and fabrics that can be used by people to **adorn** themselves. You can adorn your body by using accessories. The word 'accessory' suggests an assistant or helper. Accessories are the small things that people wear or carry, such as shoes, bags, jewellery, ties, mobile phones and watches. Accessories can be swapped around or worn only with certain clothes or at certain times.

◄ A pendant made of gold and enamel, England, around 1850

How and why people adorn themselves changes across times, cultures and individuals. In the past, it was unacceptable for some people to leave home without a hat. Today, people wear hats to protect themselves from the sun's harmful rays.

In some cultures, people paint their body or wear special things at certain times to send out a message. A wedding ring is worn because it looks nice but it also sends out a message – the wearer is married.

A backpack made of leather, plastic and metal, and a handbag made of leather, satin and metal, 1996 ◄

► A pocket watch from England, 1771

Jewellery

We do not know what the first body adornment was. It may have been body paint, or it could have been jewellery made from things such as teeth, bones, flowers or leaves.

The oldest known jewellery is beads made from grooved animal bone and teeth. They were found in France and date back to 38 000BC. Clay beads, which had been baked in a fire to make them hard, have also been found. These date back to 28 000BC.

Over the centuries, as new materials and techniques have been invented, new sorts of beads have been made. Today, you can make jewellery yourself, or buy it from someone who makes jewellery or from a shop. The same sort of jewellery can take many forms. Look at the necklaces on this page.

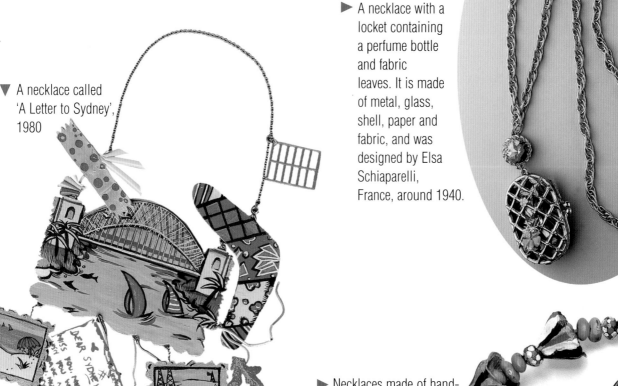

▼ A necklace called 'A Letter to Sydney', 1980

► A necklace with a locket containing a perfume bottle and fabric leaves. It is made of metal, glass, shell, paper and fabric, and was designed by Elsa Schiaparelli, France, around 1940.

► Necklaces made of hand-painted seeds and gumnuts, made by artists from Utopia, Australia, 1996

Old materials made new

'The swivel marcolite **armband**' was made by Australian artist Robyn Backen in 1988–89. The armband is made of a **bakelite** billiard ball, an electrical fitting, brass painted with copper, and gold leaf. Robyn likes to use bakelite in her work and searches second-hand shops to find it. She experimented with it and found she could cut, glue, scratch or polish bakelite. She also likes the 'memory' of what the bakelite used to be. In this armband, the memory is of a billiard ball in a pool hall.

◄ 'The swivel marcolite armband'

◄ Brooch and ring made of silver, nylon, plastic and pearl from Broome, 1997

Mutant jewellery

The '**Hybrid** Cuttings' brooch and ring above are made by an Australian jeweller, Helen Britton. Her interest is in nature and how we change it. Helen says these pieces are 'part plant, part machine, part animal – **cyborgs**, keen to graft themselves onto a passing body'.

Q **What is bakelite?**

1 Bakelite is the stuff found in the bottom of an oven.
2 Bakelite is a plastic invented by Leo Baekeland.
3 Bakelite is made of billiard balls.

The answer is on page 30.

Meet Blanche Tilden, *jeweller*

How long have you been a jeweller?

I have made jewellery for people to wear for four years, but it took me a long time to think of myself as a jeweller.

Why is this?

When I left school, I began my studies in making things from glass. During this course, I realized that I liked putting smaller parts of something together. So I started lampworking glass…

What is lampworking?

I use a very hot flame to soften the glass to change its shape. I made this machine at art school to help me get the shape I wanted in my artwork.

▲ Blanche Tilden at work in her studio, 1999

▼ Blanche demonstrating the technique of lampworking

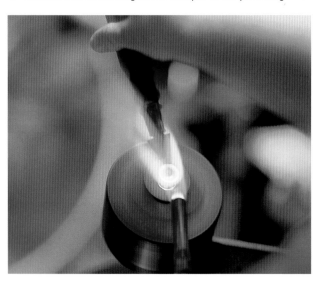

This shape is like a pulley you could find on a boat. I join these pieces to make jewellery.

Back to the first question… When you make a piece of jewellery for someone, it goes out of your hands. I put a lot of care into my work. Someone buys it because they really like the piece. It may become one of their favourite things to wear. Even though I might never meet that person, there is a connection between us.

▲ Blanche holds a piece of glass formed by lampworking.

When I started to think of these connections, I started to think of myself as a jeweller.

Were you interested in jewellery when you were growing up?

I didn't wear jewellery. I remember always being interested in how things work. If you understand how something works, you are more likely to use it. But I did not have the opportunity to do this. When I was little, it was harder for girls to understand mechanical things than boys. Girls were not brought up to be under Dad's car looking at the engine. I knew I liked putting things together but I didn't know what I wanted to do for a job.

What other training did you do to become a jeweller?

I studied gold and **silversmithing** and also worked with an experienced jeweller for two years. Many people have helped and inspired me.

How do you make your jewellery?

I use industrial glass and **titanium**. These materials are not often used in jewellery. I use tools to make the shapes and put them together to express an idea.

What sort of ideas?

I am very interested in mechanical movements and I think about how to use these movements in my jewellery. I use shapes inspired by bicycle chains, conveyor belts, pulleys, cranks and scissors. You don't have to be locked away from the world to be an artist. Your work can be about everyday life and help people think about everyday things in a new way. It took me a long while to find the work I like to do and how to do it. But it was worth it.

▼ Blanche made this neckpiece of glass, titanium and silver in 1997. It is called 'Conveyer' and is 4.8 metres long.

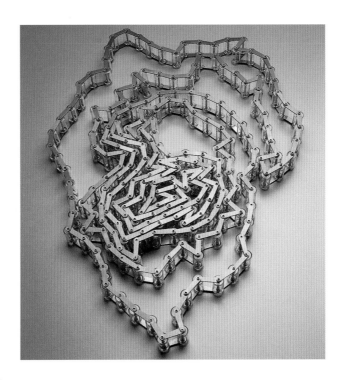

Brooches

'Widows Group' brooch

The brooch pictured right is made of objects the jeweller found such as a watch face, a Legacy badge, old jewellery and fake gemstones. Pierre Cavalan put these objects together into a new artwork. He says his work is narrative jewellery – it tells a story. It is a story that you can make up yourself. This piece is called 'Widows Group'.

Sweetheart jewellery

In wartime, some soldiers spent their spare time making jewellery. The jewellery they made as tokens of love was called 'sweetheart jewellery'. Sweetheart jewellery was made from scraps of material. The brooch below was made from the windscreen of a damaged aircraft. It was made more than 50 years ago during World War II.

▲ 'Widows Group' brooch, 1990

Q What do you think the 'Widows Group' brooch is about?

▼ Sweetheart jewellery

Sentimental jewellery

In the past, poor people carried a lock of hair from a loved one in a pouch or an envelope. Some rich people had special pieces of jewellery made of hair or to put hair in. A man usually gave the jewellery to his mother, sister, wife or female friend.

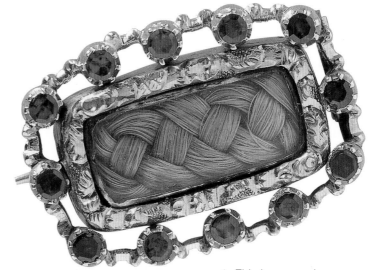

▲ This is a mourning brooch made to remember someone who has died. It is made of plaited hair, garnets, sterling silver and gold. It was made in England in 1850.

◀ Look closely at this painting of a young woman. She is wearing a brooch with a lock of hair.

Amulets

An **amulet** is any object that its wearer believes has the power to protect them or bring them luck. Amulets can be made of just about anything. Some athletes will only compete wearing a special hat, gloves or shoes. Amulets were very important to people in ancient times.

◀ Bes was a helpful household god of the ancient Egyptians. He was also thought to protect women in childbirth. Bes is a dwarf with bandy legs and bent arms. He can be found on accessories such as mirrors, pots of make-up, knife handles and amulets. This object dates back to 1500BC.

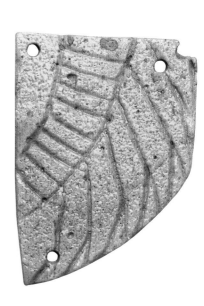

▲ These Egyptian beetles (called 'scarabs') are very old amulets made of **faience** and stone. The large blue ones were only used on a dead body, over the heart of the mummy. The holes in the scarab were used to sew the scarab onto the mummy's bandages. The little scarabs may have been worn on a ring.

Watches

The watch was invented around 500 years ago. The first watches were very heavy and hung on a chain attached to clothing. Up to 150 years ago, watches were totally hand-made. This meant that they were very expensive to buy. The first wristwatch was worn in 1914.

Citizen watch

This watch, made by Citizen, measures the seconds, hour, day, date, month, year and sign of the zodiac. It can help you locate a specific day in the past or the future. For example, if you were planning your twenty-first birthday party, it could tell you what day of the week your birthday would fall on.

◄ This is a style of watch called a fob watch. It was made by Citizen, Japan, between 1988 and 1990.

CHALLENGE 1

What day is your birthday on this year? Is it a weekday or the weekend? What day will your birthday be on in two years' time?

Ask your teacher for the answers.

Buckles

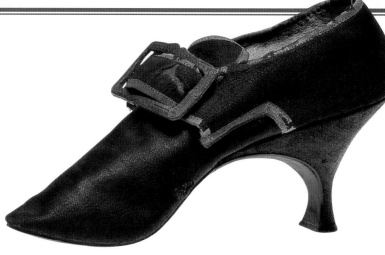

Buckles can be used to hold clothing together. They are practical – they do something – and can look good. Buckles were used as part of warriors' costumes and later as a part of armour. By the end of the 1800s, European men began to decorate themselves in different ways with buckles. They wore them on their shoes, belts, shirt cuffs and **cravats**. Women also wore buckles on their shoes and clothes.

▲ A woman's black buckle shoe made of wool, silk, linen and leather (1780–85) with a buckle made of pewter, from England around 1750

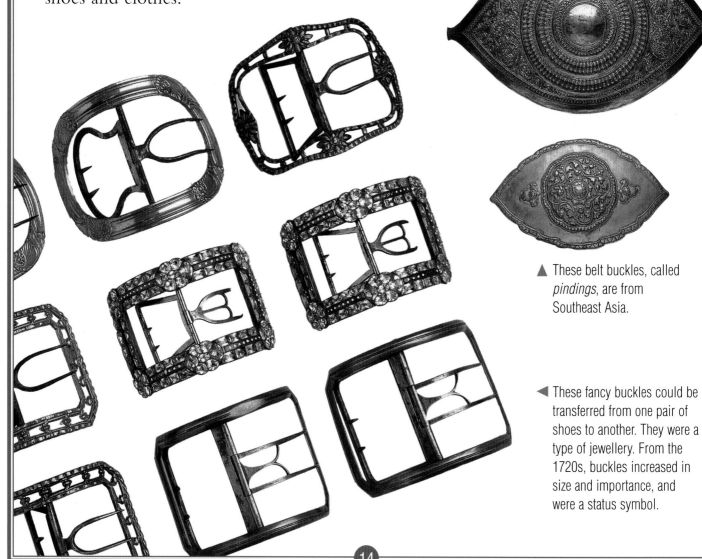

▲ These belt buckles, called *pindings*, are from Southeast Asia.

◄ These fancy buckles could be transferred from one pair of shoes to another. They were a type of jewellery. From the 1720s, buckles increased in size and importance, and were a status symbol.

Buttons

Buttons were first used as decoration in the western world during the reign of King Edward III in England in 1327. They were very fashionable in the 1600s, when people used them to decorate their handkerchiefs! Button-making began in Europe in the 1700s. Chinese and Japanese people have used knots made of silk or cotton as buttons for hundreds of years.

▲
Between 1945 and 1949, designer Gordon Andrews was sick in bed for a long period and needed something to pass the time. He decided to make buttons by hammering out pennies and then using sheet metal and wire.

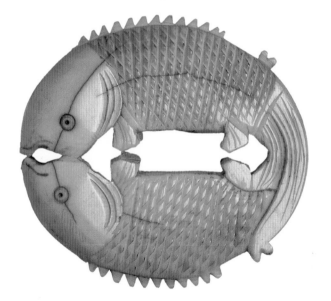

Chinese toggles

Chinese toggles were used to tie accessories such as a pouch or a bag to clothing. Toggles are a small 'block' of material, usually decorated, joined to a short strip of cloth. The toggle is pushed through a loop to act as a kind of button. Chinese toggles were made from a variety of materials including **ivory**, wood, metal, **amethyst**, **turquoise** and **jade**. Some are in the shape of lucky things.

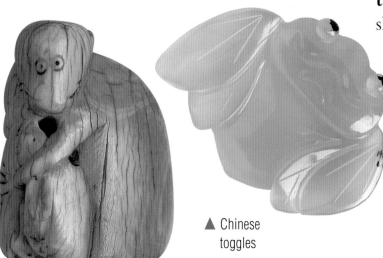

▲ Chinese toggles

Making buttons from pearl shells

These photographs from the 1930s show how pearl buttons were made.

Circles of shells called 'blanks' were cut from the shell. Cutting marks were set very close to each other to save waste.

The blanks were split into the same thickness.

The edges of the blanks were ground to smooth them into the right shape.

Each blank was turned on a **lathe** and holes were drilled in each button.

The buttons were cleaned and polished and sewn onto a card.

Collars

For hundreds of years, collars were part of a shirt or **chemise**, the way they are today. In the 1500s in Europe, collars became a separate piece of costume – an accessory. This extra piece could be made from metres of very expensive lace or it could be a simple starched collar. In the 1900s, the collar was rejoined to the shirt. There are many sorts of collars.

▲ A collection of detachable collars from around 1920

▲ A silk collar from China in the 1800s. The tapestry shows two five-clawed dragons against a sky filled with mountains, clouds and bats. The clouds and bats symbolize wealth and fortune.

► A collar made of peacock feathers from India

Umbrellas

The word 'umbrella' comes from the Latin word *umbra*, meaning 'shade'. Umbrellas, also called sun shades or parasols, were first made to protect people from the sun, not the rain.

Most umbrellas are made from ribbed frames with material stretched over them. The covering is made from equal-sized shapes cut from a larger piece of material. The sides of the shape are stitched along the ribs and the base of the shapes forms the edge of the umbrella.

▲ 'Wet afternoon' by Ethel Spowers, 1930 – a painting inspired by umbrellas

▶ Two parasols made of different materials. The parasol above was made of silk in 1865 and the one below is woven from a kind of wheat (called spelt).

Hearing aids

Ear trumpets were a simple and effective hearing aid. They collect and concentrate sound waves, and direct them to the ear. They work like a big outer ear and make sounds louder. Made in England in the 1800s, ear trumpets were popular with wealthy people.

Hearing aids today are small machines. The most advanced device is called the Nucleus Cochlear Implant System. The system has three parts: one part is implanted into the inner ear; a microphone is worn behind the ear; and a little computer, called a 'speech processor', is worn externally.

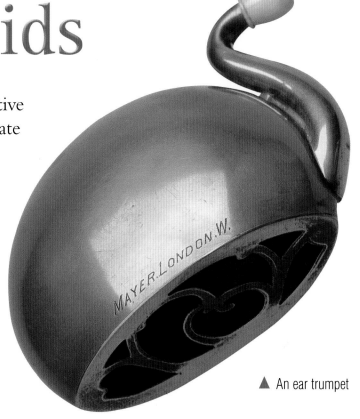

▲ An ear trumpet

▶ A drawing of the Nucleus Cochlear Implant System

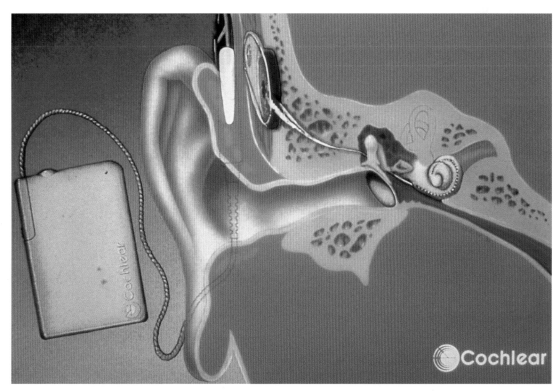

Computer sunglasses

The sunglasses pictured below contain a complete multimedia computer with camera, microphones and earphones. The sunglasses are connected to a belt with switches that can tell the computer what to do. The glasses can send e-mail, be a telephone, access the Internet, play and create music, and record what the wearer sees. For more information about computer sunglasses, go to http://www.wearcam.org/personaltechnologies/index.html

What they were wearing then

Stephen Hawking is a famous scientist. He has motor neurone disease. This means he cannot speak or move. These accessories help him to communicate his thoughts to other people:

- a computer system attached to a wheelchair – the screen is mounted on the arm of the wheelchair where he can see it
- a computer program called Equalizer™ – a cursor moves across the upper part of the screen. He selects words from the screen by pressing a switch
- a speech **synthesizer** – to change the words on the screen to spoken words
- a formatting program called TEX – this allows him to write papers for other scientists.

You can see Stephen Hawking at http://www.hawking.org.uk

◀ This is Steve Mann from Canada, wearing his 'existential computer' made in 1997. An 'existential computer' is equipment that is controlled by the wearer, always active when it is worn and seen as part of their costume.

Walking sticks

Walking sticks were a symbol of power or a sign of elegance or importance. Walking sticks were put in the coffins of Egyptian mummies. Tutankhamen had 132 walking sticks in his tomb. Walking sticks as accessories went 'out of fashion' in the 1930s but are still collected by people today.

The handles of walking sticks were often heavily carved and decorated. Animals, including snakes, were popular **motifs**. Snakes can symbolize life, death and cunning. Walking sticks also have a practical purpose. They support the wearer as they walk.

▶ This 'tiger snake' walking stick was made of wood with gold mounts between 1890 and 1938.

CHALLENGE 2

What accessory is this picture decorating?

The answer is on page 30.

Bags

A drawstring purse with orange beads and a pattern in black and
► white beads

Lucy Locket lost her pocket
Kitty Fisher found it.
Not a penny was there in it.
Only ribbons round it.

Purses were once called 'pockets'. They were joined to a tape that could be tied around the waist.

An evening bag made in the 1800s of black silk with an embroidered floral design. The bag is edged with a black cord and
► has a ribbon drawstring.

A shoulder bag, made of
▼ printed cotton, 1992

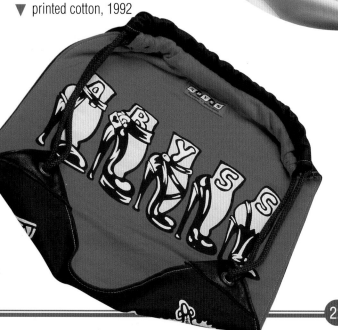

▲ A silver mesh evening bag with blue beads set on the lid, made in the early 1900s

String bags

A flax bag woven somewhere in the islands of the Pacific Ocean between 1890 and 1950 ▼

▲ This bag is made of dyed string and fluffy feathers. The string is made by taking strips of bark and rolling them across the thigh. The bag was made by Lena Yarinkura in Maningrida, Australia, 1995.

School bags

This school bag belonged to a boy who was six years old in 1932. ▼

▲ This bag was made from special cardboard in a factory. It was bought in 1938 by a girl to use as a school case. It was later used to carry her husband's lunch to work, and then as a school case for her children.

Make a bag

What you need:

- fabric
- needle and thread
- scissors
- two drawstrings
- decorations (for example, beads, ribbons, buttons)

Step 1

Cut two circles of fabric and join the right sides together, leaving a gap for turning right side out.

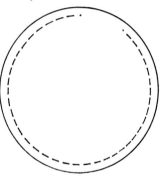

Step 2

Turn the fabric inside out so that the right sides are out. Stitch the unsewn opening.

Step 3

Ask an adult to help you make evenly spaced eyelet holes around the edge of the fabric. Mark each hole with a white pencil, then pierce the fabric with sharp scissors.

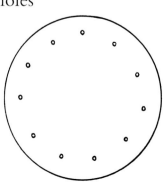

Step 4

Thread two drawstrings in and out of the eyelet holes, starting at opposite sides to create one loop on each side. Pull drawstrings to close. Decorate your bag.

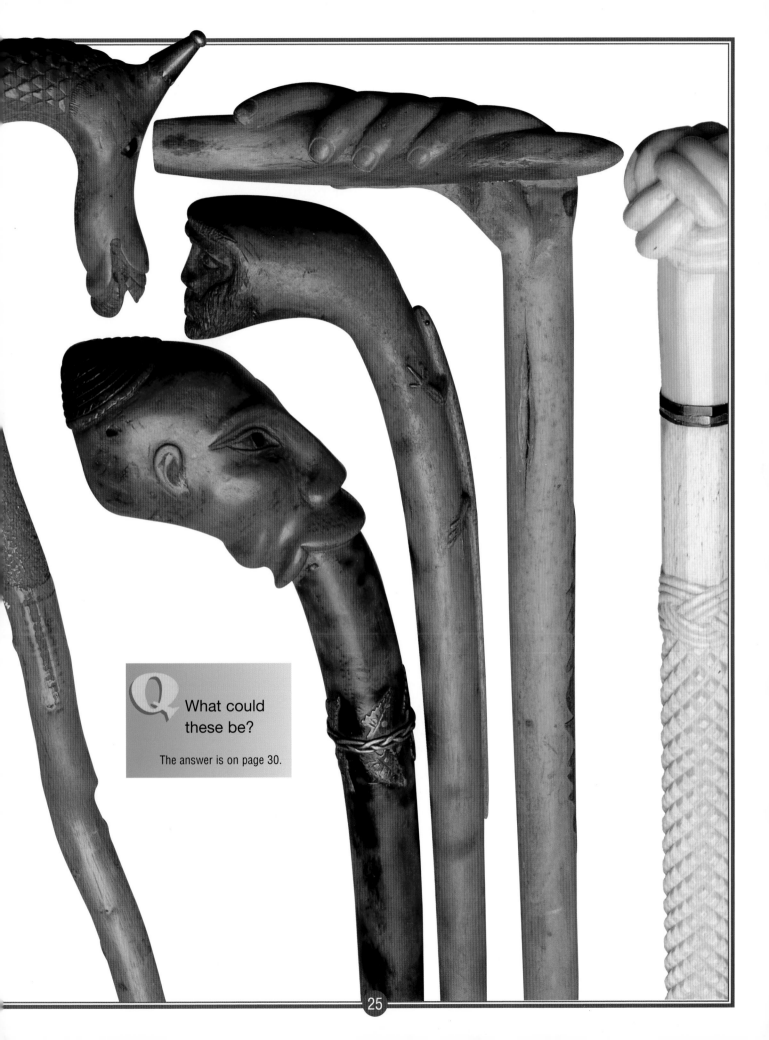

Q What could these be?

The answer is on page 30.

Body painting

Throughout history, people have painted their bodies. Sometimes it was to make themselves look fearsome when they went to war. Sometimes it was to make themselves look special for an important occasion, such as a wedding. People in some cultures painted their bodies to perform ceremonies. The designs they painted on their bodies had special meanings.

Aboriginal people are the original inhabitants of Australia. This picture was taken in 1898. It shows Aboriginal men and boys with painted bodies. They are ▼ performing a special ceremony.

Body art

▲ Stelarc – a performance artist

Stelarc is an Australian artist who wants people to think about the human body and how it may change in the future. In this picture, he is writing the word 'EVOLUTION' using his own arms and a mechanical arm – all at the same time. He moves the mechanical arm with his stomach muscles. In this picture, Stelarc is a cyborg – part person and part machine.

Hairstyles

In 1770, fashionable hairstyles were more like constructions! 'Hair-dos' combined lace, ribbons, pins, flour-and-water paste and false hair. When a woman stood up, her head and hair could be more than one-third of her height.

▶ A French fashion print from the 1700s showing a young lady in grand dress with a complicated hairstyle

Men's hairstyle timeline, 1860–2000

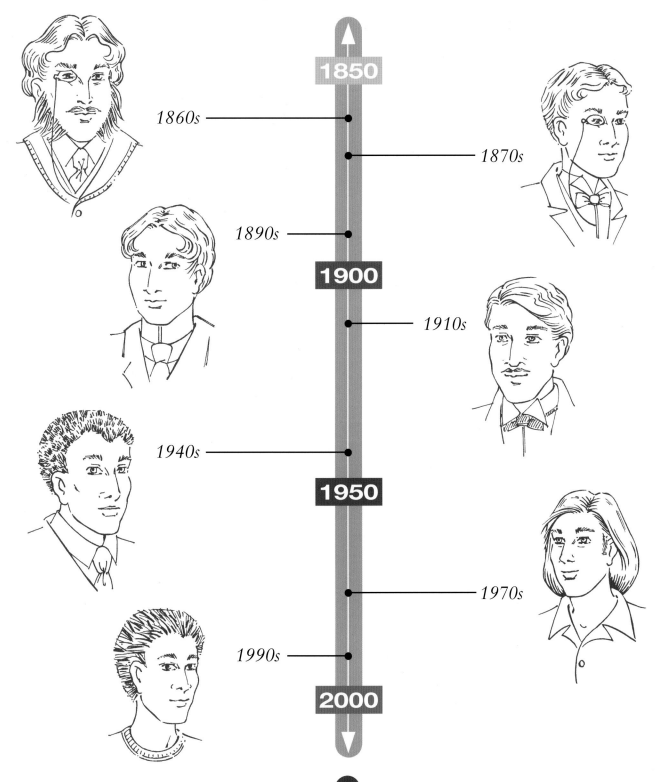

1850

1860s

1870s

1890s

1900

1910s

1940s

1950

1970s

1990s

2000

Accessories and adornment

Most people use adornment and accessories. They are part of our costume and part of our culture. Some accessories and forms of adornment have a practical purpose – we can carry something in them, or use them to walk with or protect us from the weather. Most adornment is a way of decorating ourselves so that we look more attractive. Sometimes adornment has a spiritual meaning for the wearer. Accessories and adornment are like little messages. They are saying something about the wearer.

▶ This necklace is called a 'mairreener'. It was made from kelp shells strung on cotton in Australia in 1993.

Answers

Page 7
Bakelite was the first sort of plastic. It was made by Dr Leo Baekeland in 1907. It is made from phenol and formaldehyde. It is colourful, heat resistant and easily worked.

Page 21
The picture is painted on an ivory fan made between 1790 and 1810. The picture is of a famous myth about a woman who became known as Helen of Troy. She was stolen from her husband by warriors.

Page 25
They are walking sticks.

Glossary

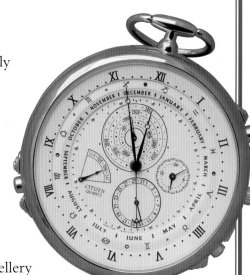

adorn make more beautiful or pleasant, or to complete a costume for a special purpose

amethyst a purple-coloured precious stone used in jewellery

amulet charm believed by the wearer to protect them

armband band of material worn around the sleeve or arm

bakelite a synthetic material made by mixing chemicals

chemise sleeveless, knee-length shirt

cravat a type of scarf, worn loosely tied at the throat, generally by a man

cyborg being that is part human, part machine

faience material made by baking or melting glazed powdered quartz into a mould

hybrid animal or plant that is the result of breeding between different types

ivory the creamy white tusk of elephants

jade a precious, usually green, stone used in carving or jewellery

lathe machine that holds and turns a piece of wood or metal while it is being cut or shaped

motif design or pattern used on a fabric

silversmithing working in, decorating and/or changing the shape of silver

synthesizer a machine that creates speech or music using electronic circuits

titanium a metal that has a strong dark grey colour and a metallic shine

turquoise a sky-blue or greenish-blue mineral used for jewellery

Index

Photo and object credits

All objects featured in this publication are from the Powerhouse Museum collection and all photographs are by the Powerhouse Museum, unless otherwise indicated below. Collection objects are reproduced by permission of the designers or makers listed. The museum acknowledges the many generous donations of objects, which form a significant part of its collection.

p3 Bakelite armband by Robyn Backen, and Abyss Studio bag by Sara Thorn and Bruce Slorach; p4 funkessentials poster by Sara Thorn and Bruce Slorach; p5 necklace and shawl by Lucy Delgarno; bags by Pacino Wan and Immi Paris; pp6/7 necklaces by Utopia Art; 'A letter to Sydney' necklace by Kate Durham, Bakelite armband by Robyn Backen, pearl brooch and ring by Helen Britton; p10 'Widow's Group' brooch by Pierre Cavalan; p11 'Anna Elizabeth Walker (Mrs Thomas Walker) nee Blaxland (1804-1809)' by Maurice Felton, 1840, oil on canvas, 74.8 x 62.2cm, The Art Gallery of New South Wales; p15 buttons by

Gordon Andrews; p18 Ethel Spowers, *Wet Afternoon*, 1929-30, colour linocut, 24.2 x 20.2cm, The Art Gallery of New South Wales; p19 graphic, Cochlear Ltd; p20 computer sunglasses photo, Professor Steve Mann, University of Toronto from *Personal Technologies* Vol 1, No 1 March 1997; p22 Abyss Studio bag by Sara Thorn and Bruce Slorach; p23 Maningrida bag by Lena Yarinkura 1995; p26 Wailwan tribe ceremony, photo by Charles Kerry, Tyrrell Collection, PHM; p27 *Handswriting* by Stelarc, photo by Ak Ro Okada for Maki Gallery, Tokyo; p28 French fashion plate from Blum, Stella, *Eighteenth Century French Fashion Plates in Full Colour*, Dover Books, 1982; p29 timeline based on information from R Turner Wilcox, *The Dictionary of Costume*, B T Batsford, London, 1992; p30 necklace by Lola Greeno; p31 brooch by Helen Britton.

Please visit the Powerhouse Museum at **www.phm.gov.au**